Penny Pulls the Plug

by Elizabeth Best

illustrated by Janine Dawson

Harcourt Achieve

Rigby • Saxon • Steck-Vaughn

www.HarcourtAchieve.com

1.800.531.5015

Characters

Penny

Goldfish

Frog

Tadpole

Contents

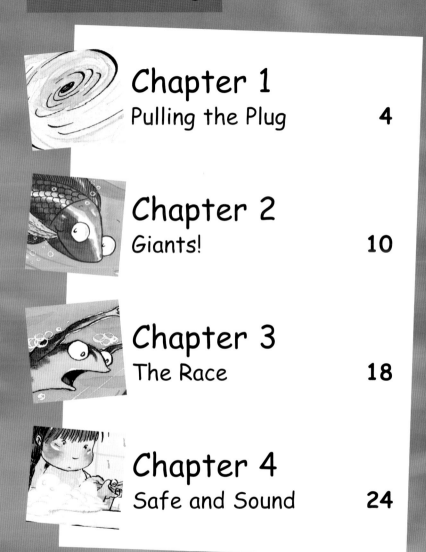

Chapter 1

Pulling the Plug

"Get out of the bath now! Pull out the plug!" called Mom.

Penny pulled out the plug.

The drain pipe slurped the water with a gush and a gurgle.

Penny's washcloth slipped along the
bottom of the bath tub. Then it shot
down the drain.

The drain caught one end of the cloth.
Penny grabbed the other.

ROARRRRRRRR!!! SCREECHHHHHHH!

Something was down there. What was pulling Penny's washcloth?

Penny shut her eyes tight and hung on grimly.

With one great gulp and gurgle, the drain pipe pulled Penny down.

Chapter 2

Giants!

Penny swished down that drain pipe at full speed.

Then Penny opened her eyes.

Penny was in a river, deep under the ground.

She had a tail like a fish. Penny was a mermaid!

A giant goldfish with big bulging eyes pulled her along. In his mouth was one end of Penny's washcloth.

On the other end, hanging on for dear life, was Penny.

Penny could see the river was in a dark, wet cave.

"Let go!" cried Penny to the goldfish.
"It's not your washcloth!"

Big fat tadpoles swam by. They were as huge as whales.

A giant frog jumped from a log. It landed with a splash.

"Help!" yelled Penny.

"This goldfish stole my washcloth!"

"We'll help!" cried the tadpoles. They joined the chase.

Chapter 3

The Race

Up and down the river they raced.

"I'll help!" croaked the frog. He kicked his strong legs.

"Make him open his mouth," said Penny.
Her arms were so tired.

"How?" cried the tadpoles.

"How?" cried the frog.

"Give him something to eat," said Penny.

"Like what?" asked the tadpoles.

"Like what?" asked the frog.

Penny didn't know what.

"Make him talk!" Penny cried.

"How?" called the tadpoles.

"How?" called the frog.

"Ask him something," said Penny.

21

The biggest tadpole asked the goldfish,
"Why are you stealing her washcloth?"

The great goldfish didn't answer.

He grinned a great goldfish grin. He shook his golden head and gurgled.

Chapter 4

Safe and Sound

Up and down the river they raced.

Penny's arms were aching so badly.

"Try tickling him!" she cried. "Tickle him and make him laugh."

The frog swam close to the goldfish.
With his long thin fingers, he tickled
the goldfish.

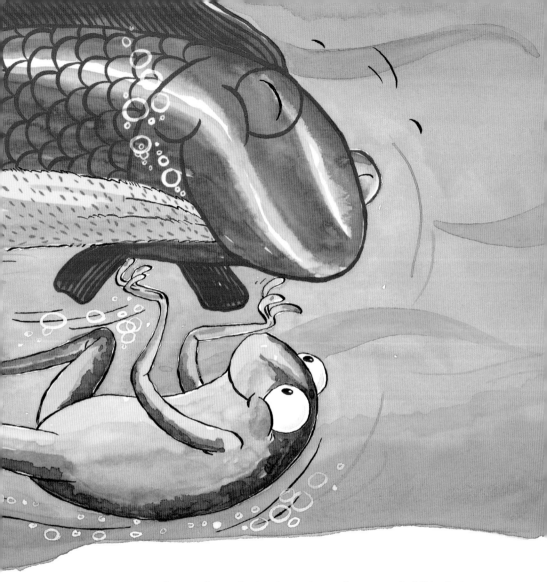

Someone laughed. Was it the goldfish?

The gurgling sound echoed around the bathroom.

Penny sat in the bathtub. All the water was gone. The washcloth was in her hands.

"Oh, there you are," said Mom.
"I thought you had gone down
the drain!"

Glossary

aching
very sore

at full speed
as quickly as possible

bulging
sticking out

echoed
a sound that
came back

grimly
seriously; in a worried way

gurgle
the bubbling sound made by water

mermaid
in fairy tales, a woman with a tail like a fish, who lives in the sea

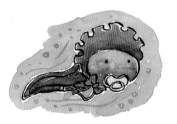

tadpole
a baby frog

Elizabeth Best

One day, when my children were little, I found them peering down the drain pipe, just after the bath water had been drained.

"There's a frog down there," said one child.

The next evening, as the plug was about to be pulled, another child grabbed her bowl of tadpoles and tipped the bowl into the bath water.

"Now that frog won't get lonely," she shouted.

I did manage to save the tadpoles, but just barely.

Janine Dawson